Hayden and the Honey Farm

Brenda Spalding
Jacqueline Paske Gill

This is dedicated, as always, to my 'Little Bug'.

His curiosity never ceases to amaze me..

"HI Mr. Albright," Hayden called skidding his bike to a stop on the gravel drive.

"Well hello to you too Hayden, does your grandma know you're over here?" Mr. Albright asked.

"Grandma sent me to see if you have a couple jars of honey she can buy. She's baking something and ran out of honey," replied Hayden.

"Oh My," Mr. Albright said, "Mrs. Albright took the last jars I had and some wax candles over to Mr. McGregor's Farm Stand.

"That's ok maybe she can make something else," said Hayden, getting back on his bike.

"Not to worry, we'll just go ask the bees if we can have some from their hives.

"Ask the bees?" said Hayden, dropping his bike. "Bees don't talk. How can we ask them for honey?"

"The bees talk. You just have to listen real hard." Mr. Albright told him. "Come on I'll show you."

Hayden followed Mr. Albright to the field behind his house. There is saw several rows of white boxes

"These are my bee hives. Each hive contains one queen bee and about 60,000 worker bees."

"That's a lot of bees. Do you ever get stung?" Hayden asked, a little afraid of getting too close to all those bees.

"I did when I first started to keep bees but I learned to talk to the bees and to be very gentle with them. Some I"ll show you how we get the honey."

As they walked Hayden asked, "Mr. Albright do my bats ever eat your bees?"

"Oh no, your bats fly at night while my bees are sleeping in their hive. They're not out at the same time."

Mr. Albright showed Hayden how to put on a bee keeper suit and helmet. Of course it was much too big for him and dragged the ground.

"First we need to use a smoker to calm the bees. It also helps to move them away from the honey frames."

Mr. Albright took what looked like a silver watering can and puffed smoke over the sides and top of the hive.

"Now we lift one of the frames out of the hive to get the honey." He lifted a wooden frame out of the hive and gently brushed the bees off."

Then he took a knife and cut off the wax honey comb the bees had attached to the frame. Mr. Albright placed the comb in a clean metal pail to catch the honey as it drained out.

Finally he placed the frame back in the hive and put the top back on.

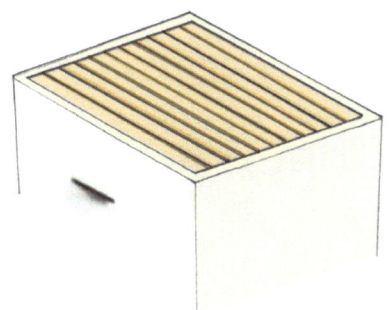

Together they carried the pail back to the house.

Hayden was amazed that the bees didn't seem to mind someone taking their honey.

"Don't the bees miss the honey and the honey comb we took from them?" Hayden asked.

"No they just keep making more. We always leave them some and never take it all," Mr. Albright explained. Now we can get some clean jars and pour in the honey."

Hayden watched all the golden honey drip slowly into the jars. Mr. Albright even put a piece of the comb in each jar.

"Thanks you Mr. Albright," Hayden said, taking the jars and placing them carefully in the basket on his bike.

Grandma was very happy to have him and the honey home safe and gave him a great big hug.

"Grandma, I helped get the honey for you. Mr. Albright showed me how. Do you think I can have a bee hive of my own? Then we can have our very own honey from our very own honey bees."

"I think you can but you need to be a bit bigger. Keeping honey bees is a lot of work and not an easy job.

How about you help me make some Honey Bee cookies? We can send some over to Mr. and Mrs. Albright to thank them for the honey."

Hayden and Grandma made lots of cookies. When they were finished they sat at the kitchen table trying a couple of the cookies with a glass of milk.

"Just to make sure they came out right," Grandma said.

Later when Mom and Dad came home, Hayden told them all about his visit to Mr. Albright's and how he helped get the honey for the cookies.

Hayden sat on the porch deep in thought. Then he turned to his grandma and asked, "Grandma, Mr. Albright said he can talk to the bees."

"That's why they don't sting him. Maybe someday I can learn to talk to the bees too?"

"Oh, I know you will my little bug, I know you will," Grandma said smiling.

From the Alpha-Bakery childrens cookbook put out by Gold Medal Flour when I was a kid. I used to love cooking up all these recipes with my mom!

INGREDIENTS Nutrition

SERVINGS 36 UNITS US

- ½cup margarine or ½ cup butter, softened
- ½cup brown sugar, packed
- ½cup honey
- 1 egg
- 1 ½cups all-purpose flour
- ½teaspoon baking soda
- ½teaspoon salt
- ½teaspoon ground cinnamon

- Heat oven to 375°F.
- Beat margarine, brown sugar, honey, and egg in a medium bowl on medium speed,   scraping bowl constantly, until smooth. Stir in remaining ingredients.
- Drop dough by tea spoonsful onto an ungreased cookie sheet.
- Bake until set and light brown around edges (surface of cookies will appear shiny), 7-9 minutes.
- Let stand 3-5 minutes before removing from cookie sheet.
- Variations:.
- Honey-Bran Cookies: Stir 1 cup of shredded bran cereal into batter.
- Honey-Cinnamon Cookies: Mix 2 tablespoons sugar and 1/2 teaspoons ground cinnamon; sprinkle on cookies immediately after removing from oven.
  Honey-Coconut Cookies: Stir 1 cup of shredded coconut into batter.

Hayden wants you to know how much you can learn about honey.

Have someone take you to the farmers market and find a beekeeper selling his honey.

Sometimes they let you taste the different flavors to see which you like the best.

What else can Honey Bees make?
Ask the beekeeper and I bet you will be very surprised.

The Buzz on Bees

Bees fly from flower to flower, sipping nectar and collecting grains of pollen. Bees have a special tongue that sucks up the nectar and a crop in their throat for storing it until they get back to the hive, where it is turned into honey to use as food.

Many plants depend on bees to spread pollen, helping them to reproduce. Flowers that attract bees are usually yellow, blue, or purple. Many bees specialize in one plant species. In areas where different flowering plants bloom at the same time, this keeps different bee species from fighting over the same flower!

Honeybees and bumblebees live in colonies or hives. All the bees in the colony work together for the good of the hive. Each has a job to do: the queen lays the eggs and the workers build the honeycomb, care for the larvae and collect the food.

Other children's books by Brenda M. Spalding

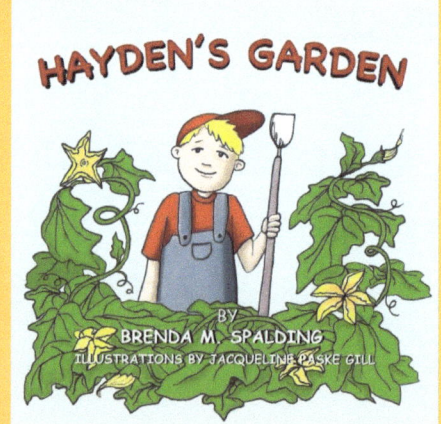

The world is just a read away.

Enjoy the journey.

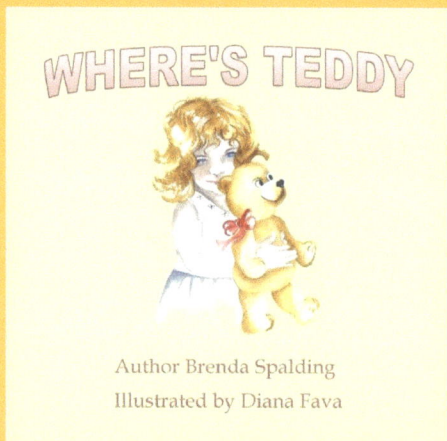

For the Adult Mystery Lovers

Thank you for the purchase of my book. I hope you enjoyed reading it as much as I did creating it.

Please check out my website and subscribe to my newsletter for information on my next new release, special promotions or where you will find me at an event.

www.heritagepublishingus.com